tranquil thoughts
on motherhood

Kattrin Davida

tranquil thoughts

on motherhood

When God thought of mother,
He must have laughed with satisfaction,
and framed it quickly—
so rich, so deep, so divine,
so full of soul, power, and beauty,
was the conception.

Henry Ward Beecher

When a woman becomes a mother, right from the outset it becomes clear that the role is not quite as straightforward as perhaps she thought it was going to be. It involves many different responsibilities, tasks and chores, and she has to think on her feet in response to each new situation that arises. Mothers all around the world have a great deal in common, but each will define motherhood according to her individual history and the nature of her relationship with it. Certain techniques and insights have been passed down to women through the generations, to help them with the challenges they will face.

Just as no two gardeners will use the exact same methods to tend their gardens, each mother will find the way that works best for her and her children. We certainly need mothers in this garden that we call Earth for where would we be without them? Human young are among the most helpless in the entire animal kingdom, born without any chance of survival if they are left on their own. There are times when the responsibility for their care can feel overwhelming, but mothers soon discover the extraordinary joy and incomparable rewards that children bring.

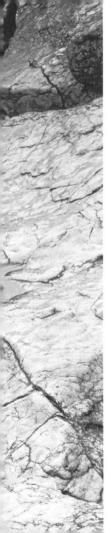

The world is full of specialists and experts in everything conceivable, but what is a mother? She must be a nurse, carer, play leader, a teacher, a language tutor, a psychologist, guide, counselor, team coach, mentor, and companion. Mothers are the first to acknowledge that in each of these professions there are trained specialists who purport to be better and more skilled than them, but it does not detract from the fact that motherhood demands these skills of all mothers at some time or other.

what is a mother?

inspiration

Where does a child's vision come from? Some believe that if a mother wants to inspire her children to write, then she should take them to the library often, and if she wants them to paint then she should fill their hands with paintbrushes and set them before an easel. Mother is there throughout the formative years to throw open the shutters and allow a glimpse of all the possibilities on offer, to provide all the understanding and support needed when the precious fruit of her womb makes a choice—whether they decide to become an astronaut or a window cleaner.

artwork

Each mother is an artist and each of our children is an exquisite work of art. Their arrival in our life changes everything. Suddenly, where before there was an empty canvas, the space has now been filled by a child, a perfect composition flooded with color and exquisite in every brushstroke. We have created a priceless masterpiece that takes its place with pride in the greatest gallery of all—life.

Mothers mold, shape,
and color their unique
creations, every day,
in everything they do.

mother knows

A mother instinctively knows how to use adversity. It's a mystery how we came to learn this, but we all have within us the capability to transform practically every tragedy into something productive. Potatoes that have become unsafe to eat can be shaped and dipped in paint to become printing blocks. A sore throat can become a "snuggle-down-day" reading and drawing in bed. Delays from here to there all become wonderful excursions into the imagination. Wherever a child has a dark cloud hanging over his or her head there is to be found a mother capable of bringing out the sun again.

no sacrifice

Mothers don't even think in terms of sacrifice. No matter what they give up to raise their children, it is always worth it.

A mother's sacrifices are many, but they are rarely noticed or even commented upon. At every level of society, culture, or civilization, when there is little food or water, the child will always be fed or quenched before the mother even thinks about replenishing herself. Her hunger is to fill her child's needs and wants. It is an insatiable state that exists from the moment she gives birth up until her dying day. She will, without exception, always put her children first. She is, after all, a mother.

Mothers provide shelter in stormy weather, refreshment in a drought, shade in a heat wave, and a warm hearth in cold winters.

no mirage

Every child is confident as they wander through life's more fertile and happy lands, but when they reach the barren deserts they need the reassurance and comfort that comes from knowing that their mother is there for them. Their mother is the oasis they will visit throughout their life, to bathe in the crystal-clear spring of her laughter and to seek shelter from the scorching sun in the soothing shade of her understanding.

Our children have an uncanny way of stretching us, making us step back to consider and tackle things that we would never have dreamed possible or within the scope of our personal capabilities. Suddenly, without realizing it, we've become chefs, artists, actors, singers, writers, dancers, fashion designers, photographers. At the flick of a switch in her child's imagination, a mother becomes not a parent but a sidekick in a two-man mission to Mars, a dragonfly, a fairy princess, or a friendly giant; she's a pop star, a professor, and a playmate.

stormy weather

Motherhood can be as changeable as the weather. Sometimes we cannot be reached for the dense fog that comes down before us; at other times we provide the sunshine in our children's lives.

We may even have developed reputations for sometimes having a whirlwind of a temper! Occasionally the actions of our children may be greeted with a cold frosty stare or we may risk drowning everybody in floods of tears, but mainly the climate of motherhood is favorable and most of the time we remain reassuringly warm, pleasant, and always with a bright sunny outlook ahead of us.

a fun fair

Sometimes we catch a mirror image of ourselves in another mother.

Have you ever stopped to watch a mother at play with her children or when she is out and about in the company of her offspring? We take on the appearance of an anthill with kids clinging to us and crawling over every inch of our body surface! We become the boat they sail on, the tree they climb, the mattress they lie down on, the punching bag for their temper tantrums, the safe haven, the comforter, the place to seek nourishment, and a wonderful living amusement arcade.

safety net

Every mother carefully constructs a small, protected world into which she first brings her child. With the new arrival safe and secure in this snug environment, she busies herself with preparing a safer, bigger world for her child that extends even beyond what she herself will live to see, just as her mother did for her, and her mother's mother before her.

thinking

From the instant a child enters this world its mother stops thinking about herself first and instead begins thinking of the two of them.

Everything now takes on twice the meaning and has twice the potential impact. This state never leaves. Even when mother and child are separated later in life, the mother will walk along a beach enjoying a sunset and think to herself how much her child would also enjoy it.

The passion of love one feels for another person, say a mate or lover, is by nature a selfish form of love when compared to the love of a mother for her offspring. A mother's love is much broader and takes in every ounce of her feelings and emotions. It does not go away, it cannot be switched off—it just keeps coming. It is fueled by the reciprocal love of one's children but there is always enough in reserve to keep it going even during those frosty periods when theirs is not so forthcoming.

perpetual love

mothers' world

Knowing what it is to be a mother is the gateway to knowing what it is to be human.

Motherhood informs and influences every thought she has, or decision she takes, each move she makes. It allows her to become intimately involved and closer to observing young thoughts and processes in action that she could not comprehend at the time of her own childhood. Now she is in the unique position of gaining a privileged insight into that other world where only those who are mothers can enter.

perspective

Young and free-spirited, many mothers today remain determined to return to work following the birth of their child only to discover that once there, they cannot bear to be apart from their offspring. It can be heart-breaking and such feelings take many mothers completely by surprise. But they swiftly realize that in the balance of things motherhood is the most fulfilling role any woman could possibly experience in a lifetime. Placing everything into perspective, surely raising another human being well takes priority over almost anything else we could imagine?

two of you

Suddenly, where before your arms were free and empty, there is now this little baby that you are nursing and everything becomes tangible fact. As you look down, a chubby little cherub face is looking up lovingly at you as your baby takes nourishment. So there you are, caught up in a tide of oneness, and nothing needs to be said or explained. It is visible and real; where there once was a woman, there is now a woman, a mother, and a child. From this point on we are going to have to learn from each other what it is to go through life together in this new relationship.

taking control

It is incredible just how much the arrival of a tiny little helpless human being can throw everything into disarray.

Out goes the old life and in comes the new. Lock, stock, and barrel. Now people will have to fight and try to win their places back in your schedule, back in your emotions, back in your life. If you allow yourself to become overwhelmed in your new role as a mother you will soon be controlled—not in control!

never-ending
story

A mother's stories, like those of all great storytellers, are told from the heart—full of detail, color, and passion. While the seafarer thrills us with stories of driving winds and freak waves, the adventurer spins yarns of far-off lands, near escapes, and mountaintop disasters, the soldier tells of battles and heroic deeds, a mother holds us in awe with accounts involving her children.

four seasons

Imagine motherhood as having four seasons. Springtime is the greeting of a newborn infant, a time of change, filled with excitement and optimism. It is gone all too quickly but replaced by glorious summer and the childhood years; years of growth, playful happiness and long carefree days. Summer seems never-ending until autumn arrives with its fascination of change and turbulence. Our children transform into teenagers, ripe and bearing the fruits of our love and labors. These can be blustery, moody days but with a little warmth they can be lovely before the beckoning hand of adulthood comes to harvest them and winter falls. The chick flies the coup and the nest is empty as they head for colleges and jobs. But motherhood continues and the cycle of seasons repeats itself in ever-quickening succession with each fleeting visit they will have with their children after that.

naturally

During pregnancy we are reassuringly told not to worry—that motherhood will come to us naturally. For some, motherhood is immediately wonderful and involving, while for others it seems like a lot of hard work.

Motherhood comes into its own for all of us when we can strike a happy equilibrium between the two, when we no longer allow the demands to outbalance the benefits and all the pleasures it can bring. To do motherhood well can and does come naturally, but that doesn't mean it comes easily and that every mother doesn't have to work at it.

43

the good shepherd

A mother is often likened to a good shepherd and her offspring to the flock of sheep. It is her job to know the right balance of discipline for each of her flock, to try to persuade them that their interests and her own are the same. And while it is the duty of a good shepherd to occasionally shear her sheep, she will not solve anything by skinning them alive!

juggling

Motherhood means coming face to face with many life-changing choices and decisions that must be made.

Will you be able to combine motherhood with marriage, let alone combine married life and motherhood with a career or work? Surely something has to go? You can't suddenly stop being a parent— there is no turning back that clock. What if your work is important to you, or you need to work? As worrying as it all seems at first, with understanding partners, relatives, and friends, life need not take any sudden downturn and many successful and productive women throughout history have managed to keep all the balls in the air, once they have grasped the basics of juggling!

symptoms

Headaches, numbness, tingling
in the limbs, chest pains,
palpitations, hyperventilating,
panic attacks, inability to cope,
impaired memory, loss of normal
interests or concentration,
bizarre or strange thoughts,
nightmares, guilt, thoughts
of jumping off a cliff, anxiety,
over-eating, loss of appetite—
happiness, happiness, and more
happiness. Congratulations!
Welcome to the crazy, mixed-up
world of motherhood.

masquerade

Motherhood is not a costume you put on for a few brief moments now and then.

When a woman becomes mother, from that moment she is exactly that. A mother! Not for periods of now and then—but for every second, of every minute of every hour, day, week, month, year, and decade for the rest of her life. There is no "time off," no sick leave, or paid holidays. The returns are not always guaranteed, but it is without doubt the most satisfying, fulfilling, and challenging thing any woman can do, and still allows a chink of opportunity to advance on other levels too.

Oh what a power is motherhood,
Possessing a potent spell.
All women alike
Fight fiercely for a child.

Euripides

strength

Children give a mother more strength and resilience than she ever thought she had. There are tales of feats so incredible as to be almost superhuman where the safety of a child is concerned. In Tampa, Florida, a child was trapped beneath the family station wagon after a jack collapsed. Without stopping to consider what she was capable of, the petite mother acted on impulse and physically lifted the incredible weight of the car in order to rescue her child.

Motherhood is the most total, full-on test for a woman.

We imagine that we will be able to organize a child into our life schedule. Then the truth arrives in child form, and everything becomes reprioritized. Suddenly, getting the mix and texture of the banana and pear mash just right becomes the most important thing and the league table of our previous priorities goes into an automatic reshuffle.

best-laid plans

catch the wind

Motherhood is a huge undertaking and needs some preparation if you are going to weather it well.

Caught in the right sail, there's an entire world on the horizon just waiting to be explored. It may seem like a gamble because it means investing everything you are and have now for a distant and uncertain future. A mother may feel that she has as much chance of controlling the outcome as she does of directing the wind, but as wayward and destructive a force as it can be, the wind can also be harvested, friendly, and productive.

57

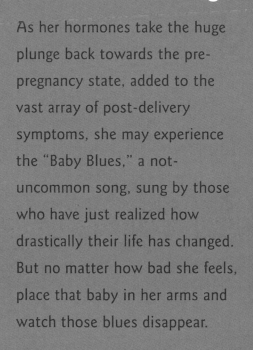

When a woman has a baby, her emotions make unfamiliar surges.

As her hormones take the huge plunge back towards the pre-pregnancy state, added to the vast array of post-delivery symptoms, she may experience the "Baby Blues," a not-uncommon song, sung by those who have just realized how drastically their life has changed. But no matter how bad she feels, place that baby in her arms and watch those blues disappear.

the blues

59

goddess

"All I am I owe to my mother. I attribute all my success in life to the moral, intellectual, and physical education I received from her."

George Washington

Every mother is a goddess to her children—a wonderful and wondrous goddess to be worshipped and adored. She is the goddess of beauty when serene, the goddess of happiness when romping in the garden, the goddess of adventure on the fairground roller-coaster, the goddess of plenty at birthdays and, above all else, she is the goddess of love. She knows what is best for her children and throughout their lives they will remain grateful that she is on their side.

in her image

"God couldn't be everywhere
so he created mothers."

The Talmud

It is interesting that God is never considered as
a mother yet motherhood is probably the best
metaphor that exists for God's parental tenderness.
With a mother's love there is nothing to disturb or
dismay her child; she teaches that all things pass,
that patience will attain what it strives for, and in
the comforting unshakable embrace of motherhood
children feel that they lack nothing.

Motherhood can seem like a new, unfamiliar, frightening territory.

Some new mothers feel anxious, stressed out, alone—even sad. It can be an exhausting time. You're afraid to relax, to stop keeping watch, even for a moment, in case something goes wrong. It takes courage to turn the tables on these feelings. Consider this: You were a baby, your mother was a baby, and hers before her. In the majority of cases more tends to go right than wrong. Try and focus upon the child and view his or her life as a happy event and an exciting experience. See the thrill of each moment and let go of the fear. Make it all memorable, not unbearable!

new experience

Every mother is a teacher where her children are concerned.

Every "why?" or "what is that?" requires an appropriate answer or some form of practical demonstration. The kitchen can become a laboratory to explore hot and cold, sweet and sour, and the garden holds a wealth of magic, birth, death, and resurrection. Something as simple as a catalog can open a child's world to a thousand new possibilities, answers, and, of course, more questions! Remember this time will not last long and what they hear from you now will be filed away deep in their own understanding for ever.

Mommy gives up smoking and mommy gives up going out to nightclubs, and mommy gives up her dance class and bridge club and downhill racing and golf— and mommy is the kind of mommy who gives up everything in order to raise her children, and when she does, there's no feeling of being oppressed. She is happy and free and for her it all feels exactly the way it was meant to be. She just wants to be at home with her children in the place where she's known simply as "Mommy."

just mommy

69

each day

If we're not careful, time can catch us out.

Once it is gone there's no getting it back again so how we choose to spend it is very important to us. We must decide early on whether it is best spent socializing in the company of relative strangers, working late for the betterment of our standing in the company, a corporate entity, or whether we would we ideally choose to pass it lovingly in the company of our own nearest and dearest. Which will we feel better about when the time comes to say good-bye to our offspring as they trundle off into their own futures? There are two ways to spell love. For a child it is spelled T-I-M-E.

back to whence
we came

Motherhood provides the exquisite and not-to-be-missed opportunity for a second stab at childhood, the chance to revisit our own childhood and get in touch with the world that younger generations inhabit. Who does not envy a child's ability to imagine, to switch off and enter into a play world where anything is possible? And what luckier adult is there than a mother who is invited into these secret worlds to partake of the magic of childhood once more?

Our children know that they can always turn to us, and we know that the echoes of our voices will always be there to help.

together forever

Our mothers never leave us and we as mothers never leave our children. We are always there in some corner of their hearts and thoughts. From the moment we set them up to take those first steps into the world we are there to prop them up whenever they seem in danger of falling. Even though our physical presence on this spinning globe may end, they will find us when they need us in the rustle of a leaf, the breeze on their cheek, a shooting star in the heavens—or the hooting of an owl at night.

be proud

The early years can be very demanding.

An infant's crying, plus the constant feeding and lifting, gets any mother down. The secret is to pause for a moment and get it all into perspective. Remind yourself in moments of despair that this helpless little human being you created and brought into the world is totally dependent upon you and that this period represents only a short time in a lifespan. Enjoy your children's dependence upon you and take pride in being able to protect them from all harm.

peas in a pod

It's a strange moment when your child begins to walk and talk exactly the way you do.

When motherhood begins there is a woman and what appears to be a tiny little alien being who's unable to communicate. Before you know it the child is wearing "your" styles of clothing, reclining on the sofa in "your" pose, and utilizing all "your" trademark phrases. You have become like two peas in a pod and it makes you wonder what else has been picked up from you!

her view

Through mother's eyes our world seems bigger, brighter, and happier. Colors glow and there is never darkness. Where we see only bad, she sees and shows us the good that's hidden underneath. She never lets the big things in life obscure the small. She sees each new day as another chance and shows us that you only get out of life what you are prepared to put into it. In her eyes, her children are the center of the universe.

Where there's defeat, a mother sees hope; she sees failure as a chance to learn, the world as full of opportunity.

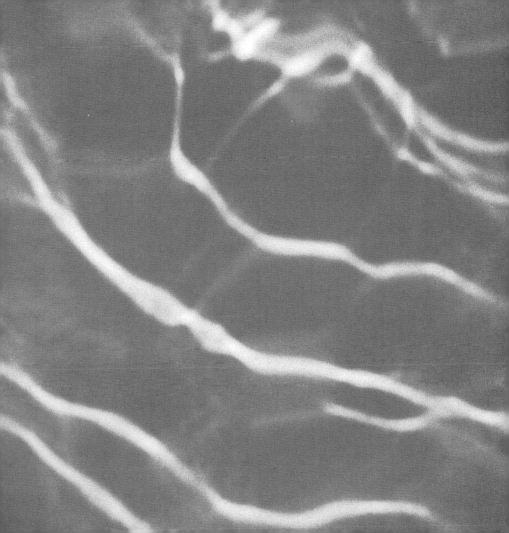

sharing

It is mother who helps her youngster learn to cope with forging relationships and friendships in life, a skill they will carry with them into adulthood. Mother teaches us how to get on with others, about loyalty and empathy, and how to develop self-confidence. She teaches us what is acceptable and unacceptable, how to communicate, to take turns and, perhaps most importantly of all, to share, for there can be no lasting relationship formed that is not based upon sharing.

In the blink of an eye our children outgrow us. One moment they are nestled up snugly beside us listening to a bedtime story, and the next they are too embarrassed to be seen with us. That face looking back at us is suddenly an adolescent with attitude who no longer seeks reassuring hugs or any kind of closeness whatsoever. No longer the smiling little face running down the hall with a finger-painting to be adored, but late homecomings and secrets. They may have changed into adults but your love and care for them does not change. We love our children at every stage of their development and cherish every moment there is.

growing up

two sides

Mothers seem to have developed a unique ability to see exactly the same things in different lights.

For instance, she hears her children laughing merrily and their happy voices seem to make all the mess okay. While her angels dance in happiness and joy, she will put aside all thoughts of tidying up after them. But when the children make the exact same mess in anger or with a bad attitude, there's hell to pay, and lessons to learn that usually begin with the phrase, "Just look at this mess!"

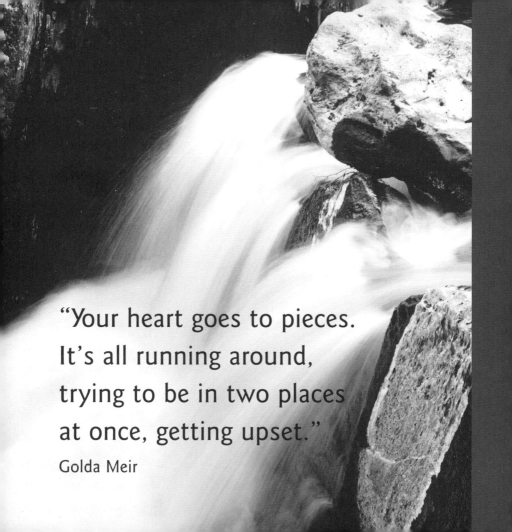

"Your heart goes to pieces.
It's all running around,
trying to be in two places
at once, getting upset."

Golda Meir

Wherever there is a **support** child performing in the school play, there is a mother prepared to sit up all night sewing a costume. Where there is a child dancing in a show, there is a mother who drives them miles every week to their rehearsals and who launders their dance gear. Where there is a child playing in the school orchestra, there's a mother sacrificing a holiday for the cost of an instrument. At a football match she's a supporter, at a charity fund-raiser she makes a donation, and at speech day she gives a standing ovation. It's natural teamwork and the baton is passed from generation to generation.

metamorphosis

When we enter the realm of motherhood, we are

nothing short of transformed. From the nine-month

cocoon of pregnancy, two new lives emerge.

One is our child and the other is our self.

Life compels people to wear
many different masks in order to
get along and fit in, but the blissful act
of becoming a mother removes all those other
masks. A total metamorphosis from who we
were—that's the other miracle of motherhood!

islands in the sun

A mother to her children is like a safe tropical island surrounded by a warm sea of love.

Her arms are the safe harbors to which they return after navigating the rougher seas of life.

And there, once they have been nourished and replenished, the time comes for the young to depart and they set off to make their own family, and find their own island. Her salt tears are the tide upon which they set sail.

many mothers

Although there is only you, all your children have different mothers. Shocked? Each of them may even have more than one! Consider it from their point of view. A toddler has the playful doting mom who answers calls of distress, who pulls funny faces, and reads bedtime stories. A pre-teenager has a playmate, a protector, a director. A teenage boy may have an angst-ridden mom who's uptight about everything he does or says, and a teenage girl has a mom who seems relaxed, focused and encouraging. Our college kids may have a mother who's brilliant, helpful, generous, always there at the end of the phone … You see? Even though they are our own offspring, only they can really let you know who their mother is.

the creator

Show to me a woman who is loyal, constant, selfless, generous, steadfast, kind, loving, encouraging, strong, unshakable, dedicated, cunning, and wise—and I will show to you a mother. Show to me a woman who is terrified at times, concerned, overwhelmed, out of her depth, lost, and exhausted—and I will show you the exact same mother. A mother is a volcano, a river, a tree, a rock, the air, the earth, an entire world. She has to be. Godlike, she is a creator, the depth of wisdom and nurturer of her children's bodies and souls. She feeds her children with herself and gives to them the wonderful gift of eternal life.

the gift of time

Children crave a mother's time more than anything else. It's a hunger that every mother must satisfy if they truly want their child to feel loved. It is not enough to lavish gifts upon youngsters hoping that will make everything alright. There is nothing that can be bought that will come anywhere near to the security and confidence that is to be gained from the implicit knowledge that you are always there for them.

thank you

Thank you, mother, for the books we've read,
The art we've seen, the vacations we've had,
The flowers we've picked,
The smells we've smelled,
The seeds we've sown, the chats, the spats,
The cares we cared, and the life we've shared.

You are
Our fortress, our shelter,
Our sanctuary, our friend,
Our tower of strength, our river's end,
Our sunshine, our beacon,
Our inspiration,
Our enduring and unfailing
Motherhood nation.

firm favorite

A mother must be capable of flexibility
while remaining firm enough to be
effective in her motherhood role.

All children require discipline in their lives if they are to get along, let alone excel. Although a mother may have the patience of a saint and a spirit of tolerance that would make even an angel blush, if she doesn't provide discipline she will have let her child down. It's not about being heavy-handed with them or issuing punishments, but about the ability to help our children recognize and understand what is and what isn't considered acceptable behavior in life.

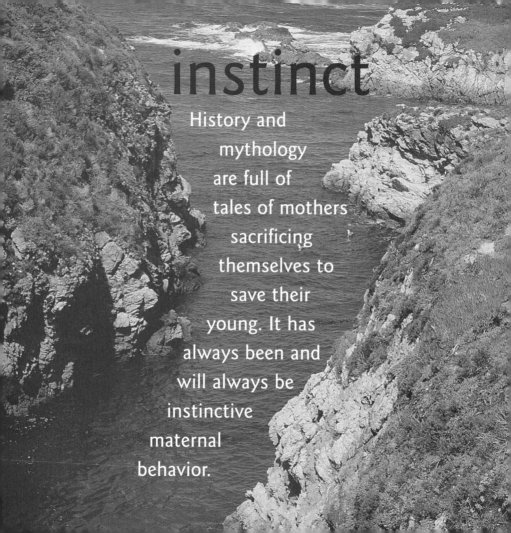

instinct

History and
mythology
are full of
tales of mothers
sacrificing
themselves to
save their
young. It has
always been and
will always be
instinctive
maternal
behavior.

A vixen will risk sacrificing herself to save her young, leading the dog pack from her lair to ensure their safety. And so it is in nature. Every female, regardless of the species, has imprinted somewhere in the fiber of their being the instinct to protect their young from danger. This "mother's instinct" is deeply rooted within us and it doesn't take much to trigger us into becoming fiercely, passionately maternal.

Nothing can compare with a mother's sorrow at being parted from her offspring.

parting sorrow

When her children leave home, a mother is confronted with all the stillness, solitude, peace, and quiet that she knew before she gave birth, and it is terrifying to her. She misses the chaos and the challenges. Then comes the blissful reunion. Instantly she is back in the company of her children, the mixed emotions dissolve and she begins to feel more like herself—she feels good again.

It doesn't take great courage or skill, or amazing feats of earning or achievement to enter the world of motherhood.

However, motherhood does require a great deal of fortitude and an unwritten promise to our children that we will give them only the very best we have to offer of ourselves at all times and for all time. It is the most challenging and demanding job that we will ever be called upon to perform, but the rewards are endless. Each child is unique, and the relationship between mother and child is truely something to cherish.

Published by MQ Publications Limited
12 The Ivories
6-8 Northampton Street
London N1 2HY
Tel: +44 (0)20 7359 2244 / Fax: +44 (0)20 7359 1616
e-mail: mail@mqpublications.com
website: www.mqpublications.com

Text © 2003 Kattrin Davida
Cover image: Grace Carlon, Flowers & Foliage
Interior images: © Digital Vision

ISBN: 1-84072-465-X

1 3 5 7 9 0 8 6 4 2

Printed in China

Note on the CD

The music that accompanies this book has been specially commissioned from composer David Baird. Trained in music and drama in Wales, and on the staff of the Welsh National Opera & Drama company, David has composed many soundtracks for both the theater and radio.

The CD can be played quietly through headphones while relaxing or meditating on the text. Alternatively, lie on the floor between two speakers placed at equal distances from you. Try to center your thoughts, and allow the soundtrack to wash over you and strip away the distracting layers of the outside world.